ETCH
A SKETCH

AuthorHouse™
1663 Liberty Drive
Bloomington, IN 47403
www.authorhouse.com
Phone: 833-262-8899

This book is printed on acid-free paper.

ISBN: 979-8-8230-0737-5 (sc)
ISBN: 979-8-8230-0736-8 (e)

Print information available on the last page.

Published by AuthorHouse 07/12/2023

authorHOUSE®

ETCH A SKETCH

PATRICIA G. CUTRELL

DEDICATION

I WOULD LIKE TO DEDICATE THIS BOOK TO MY HUSBAND OF THIRTY YEARS OF MARRIAGE: IT IF WASN'T FOR TIMOTHY N. CUTRELL. I WOULD NOT HAVE ANY BOOKS TO WRITE. ALL THROUGH OUR MARRIAGE, TIMOTHY SHARED MOSTLY ABOUT THE GOOD TIMES HE HAD, SPENDING A LOT OF HIS CHILDHOOD DAYS AT HIS GRANDMOTHER HATFIELD'S HOME, AND PLAYING WITH HIS AUNTS AND UNCLES. I HAVE ONLY WRITTEN ONE OTHER BOOK BESIDE THIS ONE THAT CAME OUT IN 2013, "FAIN NANNY FAIN." IT WAS ABOUT CUTE LITTLE RED HEADED BOY THAT LOVED TO WATCH A TRAIN EVERYDAY THAT CAME BY HIS GRANDMOTHER'S HOME IN VIRGINIA, BUT ONE DAY THE LITTLE BOY (TIMMY) DID SOMETHING THAT HIS GRANDMOTHER TOLD HIM NOT TO DO SO, TIMMY GOT PUNISHED. I WAS TRYING TO SAY THAT WHOEVER IS IN CHARGE OF US, WE NEED TO MIND THEM RATHER IT BE OUR MOM, DAD, TEACHER, AND GRANDPARENTS TOO. WE MUST LISTEN TO THEM. THE LESSON I HAD IN MIND WITH THIS BOOK IS, IT IS NOT NICE TO PLAY JOKES ON ANYONE OR SOMEONE MIGHT GET HURT. THERE WAS A LOT OF MEMORIES BEING MADE BACK.

WHEN TIMMY WAS WHAT WE CALLED "KNEE HIGH TO A GRASSHOPPER!"

WE CAN NOW SHARE THESE STORIES WITH OUR KIDS, AND THE 12 GRANDCHILDREN THAT WE HAVE. TIMMY HAS LOST SOME OF HIS AUNTS AND HIS MOM AND DAD TOO. FOR THERE ARE TWO AUNTS AND THREE UNCLES LEFT TO SHARE MORE MEMORIES WITH. WHEN YOU READ THE BOOK YOU WILL KNOW IT WAS TIMMY'S UNCLE. JOSEPH HATFIELD. WE CALL HIM UNCLE JOE THAT CAUSED SOME TROUBLE FOR "LITTLE TIMMY." WE HAVE LAUGHED SO MUCH ABOUT THE "ETCH A SKETCH" STORY, IT WILL MAKE OTHERS LAUGH WHEN THEY READ IT TOO. I DO PRAY.

A LOT OF FOLKS WILL ENJOY THIS BOOK TOO. EVEN AS MUCH THE LIKED "FAIN FANNY FAIN".

INTRODUCTION

THIS IS A TRUE STORY:

THIS BOOK IS ABOUT A CUTE LITTLE RED HEADED BOY, FIVE YEARS OLD, THAT STAYED A LOT AT HIS GRANDMOTHER AND GRANDDADS HOME IN SUFFOLK, VIRGINIA. THE GRANDPARENTS LAST NAME WAS HATFIELD. YES, LIKE THE "HATFIELD'S AND THE MCCOY'S". EVERYONE IN THE FAMILY CALLED THE CUTE RED HEADED BOY "LITTLE TIMMY". I HAVE HEARD EVERYONE IN THE FAMILY SAY THAT. "LITTLE TIMMY" WAS VERY SPOILED. I BELIEVE IT BECAUSE I AM MARRIED TO "LITTLE TIMMY".

AND HE IS STILL SPOILED! I TOOK OFF WHERE THEY STOPPED AT TO SPOIL HIM ROTTEN!

"LITTLE TIMMY" IS NOT SO LITTLE NOW. HE IS A "BIG TIMMY", AND HE HAS A SON. WE CALL HIM "LITTLE TIM" AND HE HAS A SON NAMED AFTER HIS DAD BUT WE CALL HIM EDWARD. WE COULD NOT HAVE THREE "LITTLE TIMS" IN THE FAMILY. I AM LITTLE TIM'S STEP MOM, AND I AM STEP MOM TO LITTLE TIM'S THREE SISTERS, DOROTHY, LINDA, AND PATRICIA. I LOVE TO TAKE PICTURES AND MAKE MORE MEMORIES ALONG WITH THEIR MOM DEBBIE. LITTLE TIM'S SISTERS, AND MOM LIVE IN VIRGINIA.

BIG TIMMY AND I ALONG WITH THE LITTLE TIM HIS WIFE ASHLEY, LIVE HERE IN GEORGIA WITH THEIR TWO CHILD TIMOTHY EDWARD AND SARAH LOVE. MAYBE ONE DAY, THERE MAY BE OTHER BOOKS WRITTEN ABOUT TIMOTHY EDWARD AND HIS SISTER SARAH, AND THEIR ADVENTURES OF HOW THEY GREW UP AND CAME TO OUR HOME AND PLAYED WITH THE DOGS WE HAD IN OUR LIFE AND ALL OF THE MAC N CHEESE I MADE FOR THEM.

THROUGH THE YEARS, I LOVE FAMILY AND SITTING AROUND LISTENING TO THE DIFFERENT STORIES OF EVERYONE'S CHILDHOOD.

IT WAS UNCLE JOE THAT THOUGHT OF THE JOKES TO PLAY ON "LITTLE TIMMY". ONE DAY GRANDMA HAIFIELD BOUGHT AN **ETCH A SKETCH** FOR "LITTLE TIMMY" TO PLAY WITH. "LITTLE TIMMY" SPENT HOURS AT A TIME PLAYING WITH HIS NEW TOY. "LITTLE TIMMY" TOLD HIS GRANDMA HATFIELD THAT THE **ETCH A SKETCH** WAS HIS FAVORITE TOY.

ONE DAY "LITTLE TIMMY" WAS SITTING ON HIS BED MINDING HIS OWN BUSINESS PLAYING WITH HIS **ETCH A SKETCH**, UNCLE JOE DECIDED TO PUT A PLAIN WHITE SHEET OVER HIS FACE TO PRETEND HE WAS A GHOST. THIS WAS NOT SUCH A GOOD IDEA BECAUSE WHEN UNCLE JOE WENT INTO THE ROOM WITH THE SHEET ON, THIS MADE "LITTLE TIMMY" SO AFRAID HE TOOK THE **ETCH A SKETCH** AND HIT UNCLE JOE ON THE HEAD.

UNCLE JOE RAN OUT OF THE ROOM LAUGHING AND SAYING, "OH! MY ACHING HEAD!" "LITTLE TIMMY" WAS CRYING SO HARD THAT GRANDMA HATFIELD CAME TO SEE WHAT WAS WRONG.

"LITTLE TIMMY" TOLD HER WHAT UNCLE JOE HAD DONE. "LITTLE TIMMY'S" UNCLE JOE GOT PUNISHED FOR PULLING SUCH A JOKE! IT WAS GRANDMA HATFIELD WHO SAID, "SEE SON, WHEN YOU PLAY JOKES ON FOLKS SOMEONE COULD GET HURT!" "LITTLE TIMMY'S" UNCLE JOE NEVER PLAYED ANY MORE JOKES ON "LITTLE TIMMY".

SOME OF THE AUNTS LOVED TO PLAY WITH "LITTLE TIMMY". THEIR NAMES WERE LINDA AND RACHEL. THE OTHER AUNTS ESTHER AND LUCY MOSTLY HELPED THEIR MOM IN THE KITCHEN DOING THINGS LIKE COOKING AND CLEANING THE DISHES.

WE ALL NEED TO BE CAREFUL WHEN PLAYING JOKES ON SOMEONE, WE CAN HAVE FUN WITH SOMEONE BUT ALWAYS THINK TO YOURSELF, WILL THIS OR COULD THIS HURT SOMEONE? "LITTLE TIMMY'S" UNCLE JOE LEARNED AN IMPORTANT LESSON THAT DAY, AND EVEN NOW HE HAS SAT DOWN WITH HIS GRANDCHILDREN AND TALKED TO THEM ABOUT PLAYING JOKES ON FOLKS! EVEN AS AN ADULT, WE NEED TO BE CAREFUL WHEN WE ARE HAVING FUN. THINK THINGS ALL THE WAY THROUGH BEFORE WE HAVE FUN WITH OTHERS.

"TIMMY" ALWAYS TELLS OUR GRANDCHILDREN TO BE CAREFUL ABOUT THE JOKES WE WANT TO PLAY ON SOMEONE. WHEN THEY ASK WHY HE TELLS THEM WHAT HAPPENED TO HIM, AND HE SAYS NOW HE FEELS BAD ABOUT HITTING HIS UNCLE OVER THE HEAD WITH AN **ETCH A SKETCH,** IT IS FUNNY NOW WHENEVER SOMEONE MENTIONS IT. BUT TO A LITTLE BOY FIVE YEARS OLD, IT CAN BE CRUCIAL.

Printed in the United States
by Baker & Taylor Publisher Services